T0348671

"It's amazing when an anthology of different voices still manages to feel like a cohesive, breathing whole. These poems, together, are a choir, a song of hope and longing you will feel vibrating deep in your bones long after reading. "tell me everything you know / of tenderness" this book asks of its reader, and I am here, with my chest unlocked, ready to speak of it."

— GRANT CHEMIDLIN, author of
What We Lost in the Swamp

"This collection reads like a secret, some whispered truth offered in hushed tone on the edges of a crowded room. It sticks with you that way, too. These poems, these raw and varied, diverse and vulnerable bits of ache, of joy, of sorrow, and mostly of beauty, burrow into your mind and keep the whisper going long after you've put it down. So much talent, I've never envied the judge of this contest less."

— TYLER KNOTT GREGSON, author of
Chasers of the Light

Collections and Anthologies
from Central Avenue

Central Avenue Poetry Prize 2024
[Dis]Connected: Vol. 1
[Dis]Connected: Vol. 2
Alone Together

THE
2025
CENTRAL
AVENUE
POETRY PRIZE

EDITED BY
BEAU ADLER

central
avenue

2025

Published by Central Avenue Poetry, an imprint of Central Avenue Marketing Ltd.
centralavenuepublishing.com

THE CENTRAL AVENUE POETRY PRIZE 2025

978-1-77168-394-4 (pbk)
978-1-77168-395-1 (ebk)

Published in Canada
Printed in United States of America

1. POETRY / Anthologies   2. POETRY / Subject & Themes - General

1 3 5 7 9 10 8 6 4 2

Dear Reader,

This is the work of many talented hands and many labors of love. Like people, no two poets contained in this collection are exactly alike. Their work is ample as it is tremendous, and though this volume is little, it is infused with a vastness that plucks at the threads of the wide and tumultuous tapestry that is humanity.

Our first edition of the *Central Avenue Poetry Prize*—an ambitious undertaking—was a triumph. With nearly 150 submissions from poets all across the world, it was with a Herculean effort that we selected the right ones to be published. One would think with another year of experience under our belts, this edition would be somewhat easier to produce; that submissions would be simpler to pick through, that we'd know what makes the best or the most beautiful work. It was not.

The act of creation is an intimate one, and sharing those creations is no different. Poetry is like a window: we see into the poet's head and very likely their heart. But beyond this, it's a mirror. In peering into another's heart, we also catch a glimpse of our own. That's the burden and blessing of art. It has the power to change and inspire, to reflect and to captivate. And that is something worth commemorating.

This collection has been separated into three sections: Journeys, where we see evolutions of the self, the cumbersome venture of "becoming," or the art of discovery; Phantoms, in which the poets will regale you with tales of lost loves, enduring grief, and the tender act of remembrance; and finally Bonds—the crux of the human condition, and the thing that ties us all together.

I consider myself fortunate to have seen the work of so many different people; to be invited into their kaleidoscopic souls. I hope you feel the same. Thank you to everyone involved with this beautiful series.

This isn't a book about you, but a book about all of us.

—*Beau Adler*

CONTENTS

BONDS

The 2025 Central Avenue Poetry Prize

JOURNEYS

THERE IS NO MASTERCLASS IN POETRY

it simply lives in you
like a teenager
on the verge of eighteen

until it finds the courage to
leave

until it rebels from
your body

pushes its way
out the door
of your mouth

and leaves it
unhinged

MICHELLE ARMITAGE is a poet living in Spruce Grove, Alberta. She finds deep purpose by
sharing open and honest reflections of life in its most impactful moments. Her work explores a wide
range of themes, including nostalgia, inner strength, self-reflection, resilience, and motherhood.

SIXTEEN

I read somewhere
that we are all
nesting dolls
Every age
we ever were
still tucked inside us
Today
I was sixteen
and every ugly
insecurity
I knew back then
reared its head
and fought with me
until I lost
and the tears
flowed
Tomorrow
I may defeat them
with strength
I've gained throughout
the years
But it's only
banishment
to a further corner
of my mind
until the next time
I'm sixteen

CATE MCMINN is a Minnesota-based poet. She is married with four kids, three cats, eleven dogs, and a snake. When she is not reading or writing she enjoys being part of her local community theatre, coaching high school speech, showing horses, and training sled dogs.

SOMETIMES THE BURNS ARE WORTH IT

I regenerate in ash and soil and as
tempests rage, stars sing to me each night,
invite me to play.
Earth births blossoms and spoils
and ripe fruit juice is sticky
on July's sweaty, sun-stained lips.

I taste lightning dust
on my parched tongue.
A storm's fiery bolts bury
in my dark irises. I become
a girl of thunder, a girl of summer.

Kiss me under a new moon, taste
mangos and blackberries and
thick, sweet honey.
My bees buzz in my throat,
my body a temple to worship,
a queen they are bound
to guard and protect.

Nature's secrets burn in my fragile
bones. The girl I was before my
inferno drifts, a phantom fading
into heat's blacktop haze.
And well, I'm proud of
the woman my burns raised.

AMY E. VAUGHN is a poet from New Jersey. With over fifteen years of writing experience and a
BA in English literature, her work explores womanhood, mental health, and the human experience.
She indulges in books, coffee, wandering the globe, and spending time with her cat, Baya.

LINEAGE

trace the face
a composite synthesized
some voices all bone

structured like intelligently designated
lines presented generationally generated
pieces unwhole

devising several waypoints
trailheads tell a backstory
it went like this

    one land then another land
    one bridge then a tunnel
    one gradient fading

never straying from its natural
state
    as one fades a window
blooms as buds become gardens
become home

CHRISTINA M. RAU's poetry collections include *How We Make Amends* and the Elgin Award-winning *Liberating the Astronauts*. She serves as Poet in Residence for Oceanside Library (NY) and offers yoga-writing workshops. Her poetry airs on Destinies radio (WUSB) and has appeared in various journals. When she's not writing, she's watching the Game Show Network.

TENDER FLESH

Someone tell me, how is it the clementine
untangles itself so easily? The punch of a

single fingernail and it slips out of its thin
citrus skin like a molting corn snake or a

lickerish lover, giving itself so willingly to the
ripened breeze. And tell me, please, how

might I be more like the clementine? I'd like to
shed my battered hull and float

freely with the pappus and the seabirds—
to trust the wind that chooses me and maybe,

eventually, be brave enough to face whatever tender
flesh lay under my own puckered skin.

ELISE POWERS is a Seattle poet with a BA in English literature. Her work explores the
subtleties of the human experience, spanning themes of identity, loss, and belonging. She has
worked in copywriting and editing but dedicates herself to poetry. Elise enjoys sitting beachside
with a book and an Americano.

LIBERATION

i often think
about the version
of my mother
i only caught glimpses of

like when she was getting ready
to go out with her friends
smiling at the mirror
in her dressing room

joking and laughing
with other women
at kitty parties

listening to hindi songs
singing as she ironed
everyone's clothes

playing badminton with me
attempting to teach
her not-so-athletic daughter

i wonder
if i will ever
get to know her more

i wonder
if she will   ever
get to know   herself   more

TANIYA GUPTA, a poet from Punjab, India, now resides in Toronto, Canada. Her debut, *What Will People Say*, was featured in Indigo's favorite poetry list. Passionate about creating safe spaces for women to share their stories, her poems reflect on the lives women live and the lives they don't get to live.

MEDUSA

i was punished for love
and now they fault me
for loving to punish

don't point and cry, "Monster!"
at your own creation

Perseus can have my head
i've got a garden full of them

EMILY JEAN is a singer/songwriter, photographer, and poet from Amherst, Virginia, currently residing in Charlottesville. She began writing poetry in elementary school and continued to develop her passion for performing and writing in college, where she studied music industry and vocal performance with a concentration on songwriting.

MEDUSA

Isn't there a bit of
Medusa in all of us?
A monster, waiting
To be unleashed.

Turning our hearts
To solid stone,
Trapping our gazes
In moments of fear;

Isn't there a bit of
Medusa in all of us?
A hidden rage,
A reason to be afraid.

AUBREY MONSON grew up in Farmington, Utah. She loves to travel and water-ski, and has
been writing poetry since she was thirteen.

DID I METAMORPHOSE WRONG?

My hometown is a bruise on my thigh, and it won't quite let me forget it. You've settled to a low hum in my chest, like a radio filling the air from the corner. I don't change the channel anymore. You're not here, so I'll keep you safe in a memory. Time softens the blow; it's the kindness you could never show me.

The new house has a mystical feel to it: no more layers of time stacked ocean-deep. I'm not used to a place that isn't swimming in gossamer strands of web that catch my attention at every step, clinging like a child to their beloved mother. I don't know the grocer, the elementary school is a stranger. The roads haven't etched themselves into my veins, and the strange view the horizon cradles still catches me off guard. Everything's changed, yet most days I rise from the warmth of bed feeling like I've stepped into a ghost of myself. A glove, a facade—an echo.

I wish that some right decisions didn't ache as deep as the wrong ones.

I wish how much I've changed didn't help me zoom in on what's left.

I wish. I wish. I wish.

Change comes at a cost—my soul is lighter, I smile more often. Change comes at a cost—you're no longer here beside me. Some days I don't know which of these hurts me more.

Does the butterfly miss what it was before? Was the first thing it noticed the flaws in its wings?

LEAH SHADLE is a poet and writer currently studying paleobiology at Bowling Green State University. Her work is inspired by grief, hope, and a curiosity and wonder for the natural world.

LISTEN, IT'S VERY SIMPLE.

I am morphing, not someone who does not GAF.
If there is an F to G, I am not G-ing it.

Cold, unfeeling. I am like a starfish,
something even grosser, probably.
An urchin, a mussel. An oyster.

Oysters do not compulsively check Instagram stories.
I get it, man—you squeezed all the good stuff out of me
and it was too much for that little cup you got there.
I'm not cleaning up the mess of me!
Sounds like a *get a bigger mug* problem.

I am under no more illusions,
Chris Angel rehabilitated.
It rained yesterday. I had a suspicion
that this wouldn't work out
and look at me being all right and shit.
I should be a weatherman. It rained yesterday.

I should bet on the ponies.
Then at least I'd make some money
when something runs away from me.

Look—there are not always gems
to be found in the dirt of us.
Sometimes we are doomed to
passively like each other's photos
until one of us dies.

My grandfather wrote letters
from the trenches of France,
but you're right,
that was before grindset culture.

This was not a waste of time.
If I must give every last drop of me
in order to know what I should walk away
from then I will walk away empty every single time.

I wrote my first love letter to a blackberry bush and
she is still thinking about it.

I have been wailing about how good it feels to miss someone
since I could get air through these pipes.
Tell me if you are hearing me.
I am a big rind to pick around,
I am a big pit to spit out.

I understand that the concept
of love is sometimes more of a tar and feathers
situation. I'm not sure how much more I can
say about it,
that is,
until I take another breath.

SOPHIE MORELLI is an Adirondacks-based poet with a bachelor's degree in English literature
and writing and a master's degree in English education, both from SUNY Potsdam. She was an
Anne Labastille resident in the fall of 2023 and has work featured with Querencia Press. Her
poetry collection *Fathom* is out with Bottlecap Press.

PINK PARAPHERNALIA

i didn't use to wear primary colors outside
of the house   candy red,
cobalt blue and carnation yellow
were forbidden words unspoken between
the kindred heterosexuals crawling on
thoroughfares and byways
gothic subtleties were my denomination
thrifted mythologies of ll bean and faded fruit of the loom
were all i could fathom
for over half a decade   when
the vibrant veneers of childhood proved
too sharp after chipping them on some assholes in class

when i left my barber one day i spotted
a white man in a flamingo pink skirt   walking
his dog down my street   after twelve years of the
same hairdresser without so much as a glimmer
of gay paraphernalia   in the punjabi market
i tossed my gaze in his direction and did not
stop staring until he was a speck on the pewter
sidewalk, magnifying my incessant desire to ask
the age-old question of whether i wanted
    to be him
    or be with him
    and the glaring perplexities of gradual
retrograde in my nape of the grove   when all india
sweets & restaurant is forced to move after over twenty
years   where does the skirt fall on the bedroom floor?
where do i hang my pink and purple
caterpillar fleece
when a tim hortons crushes your windpipe and you're replaced
by five floors of luxury apts that only white ppl
can afford?   there's a tracheal scream

and separate entrance which you're now flagrantly aware of
and i'm afraid it's locked for flaming
homosexuals   dressed in other colors

WREN RUSIĆ is a Vancouver poet whose work introspects queer and BIPOC ways of life as
modes of resisting neoliberal marginalization. Wren is interested in dismantling metropolitan
fallacies by utilizing reflections of mental health, pop culture, and raw self-truths. Besides poetry,
Wren enjoys films, fashion, painting, and penning novels.

FAIRY TALES

the fairy tale i know
that one of
abandonment with each mistake
betrayal with each success
disownership with each independent decision
ostracization with each self-expression.
it's not like that now, maybe
or never was, you say.
and now i have
a tale of my own,
of acceptance for who I am
of love for what I do
of unwavering support for what I dream.
but it's just a fairy tale I don't believe
because the story that never was,
or maybe once was, or maybe always was
is the one that lives in my marrow
the only tale i know
to be true.

EMMA J. WEN is a first-generation immigrant, an eldest daughter, an artist, a scientist, and a surgeon. She is a passionate advocate for mental health and writes about the struggles that arise when family values, cultural norms, and societal expectations clash with one's own individual identity.

HRT IS ALCHEMY

i start by dissolving a little blue pill
underneath my tongue twice a day,
then three times a day, before switching

to weekly injections. it feels a little like a ritual, a
little like magic, like i'm placing an offering
on the altar of a goddess i worship, except the goddess

is me and i am her because i pray to no man,
no storybook savior. if you want something done right, you
must do it yourself, so i draw 0.16 milliliters

of the elixir of life into a syringe and i plunge
it into my body. i swallow the sun and the moon, i
watch myself become golden, perfected.

i realize that this right here is my magnum
opus. not a poem, not a masterpiece, not my body of
work, but me.

i am the poem.
i am the masterpiece.
i am my greatest work.

PARKER LEE [she/her] is a trans woman poet, and the author of *coffee days whiskey nights* and *the starlight she becomes*. A midwestern transplant, Parker resides in New Jersey alongside wife and poetess amanda lovelace (and their three cats), where she can be found drinking way too much coffee, and waxing autumnal every single day.

COCKTAIL QUEENS

All of my past selves are cocktail queens
spinning madly in a crowded living room.

My goodness, what a pretty necklace.
Just pop another lime into that glass.
Why yes, I'm still in Brooklyn.

People are opportunities
to demonstrate charm.

All of my past selves are so digestible
swallowing tight opinions by the cheese board.
From across the party I watch my girls
they laugh at acceptable volumes
they shimmy between truths
they gallop around the perimeter of my knowing.

Parties are opportunities
to be ever so lovely.

All of my past selves look beautiful tonight
but my girls will spend the whole evening
waiting for someone to tell them so.

SARAH JOYCE is a poet and middle school teacher living year-round on Martha's Vineyard. Her poetry explores the weight of womanhood in an increasingly digital world. She received the Director's Fellowship from MVICW and has been featured in the *New York Times Metropolitan Diary* and *MV Times.*

DON'T BELONG TO ME

Don't belong to me
For I don't belong to you
I belong to the sun at noon
And the late night moon
I belong to the desert sand
Which will always slip away from your hand
I belong to the ocean, vast and deep
And the mountain that is too steep
I belong to the late evening mist
And the rose that the morning dew kissed
I belong to every breath that I breathe
And to the soil underneath
I belong to your heartbeat
And the pain of love that is so sweet
I belong to this universe
Like a sacred holy verse
Don't belong to me
For I don't belong to you

SHEFALI DANG is a Toronto-based poet, who lives with her husband, two kids, and a very furry dog. She discovered her love for words and rhymes when she was in high school; that is when she realized that when the two came together, they could create beautiful stories and vivid imagery. Her lyrical verses effortlessly weave tales of love and life. She is the author of *Blush*, a poetry book.

THE ART OF STANDING STILL

In a city without soul,
tell me everything you know
of tenderness.

Most days I struggle
to stay afloat, but you—
you make living look effortless.

Teach me how to breathe
in a world that tells us not to rest,
not to create, not to dream.

Show me where you find space
to tend to the worlds within.

Teach me the art
of standing still.

ANA DEE (Jovana Đermanović) is a confessional poet from Serbia, currently based in Ontario,
Canada. Her work delves into themes of love, loss, and self-exploration, capturing raw emotions
with a tender voice. Her debut poetry book is *Untouched*, and her poems have been featured in
various literary magazines and anthologies.

IN ORDER TO SLEEP AT NIGHT

Forget the name of bliss.
Give up the slivered chance
you've fought for all your life.
Cancel any closely held belief
having to do with attaining
anything of immaterial value.
Erase from memory all
traces of summer's teeth
effortlessly sliding into
a ripe rosy peach shared
on the grimy dock with
the wobbly wooden seat
where the night tasted of
circular starlit vibrance.
Matriculate each fragment
of your vain inventions
until they write a forlorn
trumpet solo on a jazz album
that was never pressed to vinyl.
Try to remember the name of
the last thing you wanted and lost
after which you felt a secret
relief in comfortable failure.
Pretend nothing matters
when everything does.

JOHN WEIRICK is a writer in Minneapolis whose work has appeared in magazines and online
publications with millions of readers. His range of writings include a book, poetry, award-winning
songwriting, and marketing copywriting for start-up brands and multinational corporations.

REACH

the warm tide just after sunset
as if the sun has truly fallen
into the sea
and here we are swimming in her rays
I dare to believe
the sun has dreamed up
another way to touch us

TIFFANY THIELE is a former musical theater and cruise ship performer, and spent her younger years traveling the world. She now lives and writes in Nashville with her family and dabbles in real estate home staging and interior design.

PHANTOMS

GHOST APPLES

Our family tree,
with its hardened limbs,

stands ice-covered, sparkling
from freezing rain.

Our coat of arms
are ghost apples—

those who remain
when the delicate fruit

rots and slips down
to earth, leaving behind

its hollow, fragile shell
hanging like a glass

chandelier, still glittering
long after the party ends.

I wonder if our apple tree—
like phantom limbs,

or lucid dreams—
remembers who

each fallen apple was,
and that is why

it can't let them go.

AMY LEVITIN GRAVER (she/her) is a writer, poet, artist, baker, and marketing professional based in Connecticut. She is pursuing her MFA in poetry from Southern Connecticut State University while working full-time as Creative Director at Yale Engineering. Amy also serves on the Board of the Connecticut Poetry Society and is completing her first book.

COMPOSTING

Half-eaten
half-alive
They didn't expect you
to survive
with your heart on the outside
of your chest
but you buried the
parts they left behind
too-chewy-too-tough-too-much
in the earth
to breathe with the spores
and be nourished by rain.

Every now and then
a soft pity visits you
nibbles at your rib cage
like the worms
a reminder that you are
part flesh
part soil.

How can you know
what the future holds
you've never
seen her hands
only felt seed-sprouts
brush by you
as they reach for the warm light
knowing
it's your time soon
it's your time soon.

ANNAH SCHEPERS (she/her) is an emerging poet from New Zealand. Holding a BSc Hons in psychology, her art is inspired by a reverence for nature, spirituality, and her experiences as a queer woman.

4:45 A.M. HAUNTING

Hello, darling.
I am the guardian of your shame.
Do not be scared of my direct eye contact
this will only burn for a little.

I have brainstormed a fair number of
solutions to the problem
but, first
you will be required
to call everyone in your contact list.

Ask them
How are you *really?*

As for getting rid of the haunting
remember, there is no such thing
as a stupid question
only one that does not get you
where you wanted to go.

SARAH JOYCE is a poet and middle school teacher living year-round on Martha's Vineyard. Her poetry explores the weight of womanhood in an increasingly digital world. She received the Director's Fellowship from MVICW and has been featured in the *New York Times Metropolitan Diary* and *MV Times.*

I STILL CARRY YOU

When you left
the world fell mute.

a hollow of silence
and static.

your body—so small.
so heavy.

but what else are we
to do with bone

but give it back?

what else are we
to do with memory

but hold it?

I carried you then.
I carry you, still.

LAUREN LEVI is a queer poet from Birmingham, England. Her work explores the highs of love, the lows of heartbreak, and the journey to mental health recovery. Writing since her teenage years, Lauren finds poetry to be a cathartic experience to help put words to feelings which can be difficult to say out loud. This poem also appears in Levi's collection *You Bury Me*.

MY TURN

When my turn comes, pay
no priest. Make
no religious overtures.

Say my name.
And when you do, cry
or scream, laugh or dream
of days we spent
in reverie, writing our own stories.

Tell our glories, record
them for each one who chooses
to mourn me.

If all I leave is stories
to replace the hole carved out
by grief, then I will rest blissfully
knowing that a journal full of me

lives on in your memories.

STEPH PERCIVAL is an Atlantic Canadian writer, mom, and designer. Her work has been
featured by Swim Press and Small Leaf Press. She's currently seeking publication for her debut
poetry collection, when she's not swimming in her TBR pile or being walked by her sheepadoodle.

APOCALYPSE MEANS NOTHING
after Franny Choi

after the first one
like when a word means nothing more
than garbled sound when repeated

acknowledge: all language is
garbled sound agreed upon

tabletabletabletabletabletabletablet
ableabletableableableableableabe
caincaincaincaincaincaincaincain
cancancancancancancancacancant:

an endofdays philosophy
sounding like a bomb sounds
sizzling down to detonate

label the luggage APOCALYPSE
feed it to the dumptruck tip it off
the bridge. nothing has changed.

the material weight like a private
view of a public space existing in
mind as well as on the map only
now the map offers no straight
lines only detoured fragile
borders deliberate and exact

apocalypseapocalypseapocalypse
apairoflipsapockoftipsapailofsips
apouchofdipsawhaleofhipsanailof
nipsapopofpipsapileofripsripsrips
ripsripsripsripsripsrrrrrripppppsss
we all fall down
a   gaping   hole

and still
it still means nothing
and nothing has changed

CHRISTINA M. RAU's poetry collections include *How We Make Amends* and the Elgin Award-winning *Liberating the Astronauts*. She serves as Poet in Residence for Oceanside Library (NY) and offers Meditate, Move, & Create workshops. Her poetry airs on Destinies radio (WUSB) and has appeared in various journals. When she's not writing, she's watching the Game Show Network.

MAKE A BROTH FROM MY BONES

Make a broth
from my bones,
call it holy,
call it heavenly,
call it anything but
what it is.

Call this poetry,
the way I nourish you,
the way love's
keeping you alive.

Make a broth
from my bones
and drink from it deeply,
seize the ritual of warmth,
trap the hope in your heart.

Stand silent at my grave,
carve the stone with my name
in the rain-slicked night,
beneath the cloud-clotted sky.

Make a broth
from my bones,
stir it slow,
let it languish
on your tongue, lover.

Harvest eternity,
the golden drip of honey
from the marrow of my soul,
let it resurrect the dreams
long buried deep below.

SHELBY MARIE is a poet from Ontario, Canada. She weaves the ordinary into magic with her words and is the author of *To Walk on Moonbeams*. Shelby loves antique things and everything that autumn brings. When she's not writing poetry, you'll often find her curled up with a book or journaling.

MISS CARRIAGE

I slid in quietly, nestling next
to the bundle of cells
as they tumbled around each other
becoming.
I licked the ever-evolving cluster
and the taste was enough to know
I needed to make it mine.
Each pump of that miniscule heart
drummed my desire for more.

The black orbs of my eyes
searched the terrain
of what wanted to be
nostrils, nose, neck.
The map of child became
a country to conquer.

Reconnaissance missions at first—
a few drops of blood—
no cause for alarm.
But oh,
I howled with laughter
the night I struck strong.
Clenching sharp fist
around the bulge
of your dreams,
squeezing the sponge
of life dry.

In that last long ache
I slipped out unnoticed
in the lump of your bleeding love.

Your useless tears baptized me.

MARY DAVINI is a poet, mother, sister, daughter, friend, and novice (but enthusiastic) birder. She is continuously inspired by the natural world and loathes being indoors. Mary currently resides in North St. Paul, MN, with her husband and three incredible daughters, and a small menagerie of pets.

DREAM DEBRIS

The article said when neurons fire
through the dormant limbs
some wild fraction of a pulse
alights a nerve bundle;
a muscular shock erupts.
The brain learns the body
as dreams get born,
corporal network secrets
filed under twitch and twist.
Bridge the tiniest chasm
ruptured, unknown.

Well, the brain is trying
to learn a second body now,
investigating all the ancillaries;
a student posture taken,
study for the pop quiz.
So take me dreamscaped,
use the sensate body map
where I'll become one again.
Perhaps this night
will prove what else
dream debris and
that wild fraction can do.

JOHN WEIRICK is a writer in Minneapolis whose work has appeared in magazines and online publications with millions of readers. His range of writings include a book, poetry, award-winning songwriting, and marketing copywriting for start-up brands and multinational corporations.

ELEGY

In the wood-panelled room,
my mother echoed the nurse's *shouldn't
be much longer*. When the doctors
entered, I bowed my head toward the black
stare of coffee. Their luminous
coats outnumbered my mom and me—
shrunk into plastic chairs. I slunk
into a corner washroom's dim
fluorescence. My eyes, his eyes
in the dull
mirror.

MAUREEN ALSOP, PhD, is the author of several full collections and chapbooks. She is the winner of the Tony Quagliano International Poetry Award, Harpur Palate's Milton Kessler Memorial Prize for Poetry, and The Bitter Oleander's Frances Locke Memorial Poetry Award. Her debut novel is forthcoming through Erratum Press.

MAMMOGRAM

As the plastic paddles come together and
flatten my breast, I think of my mother.

Afraid to ask for love, her every ailment
proves a way to get it.

Pity wears a mask of truth and she pretends
she doesn't notice.

(Take a breath, hold it)

Stepping away from the machine, I think
about how no one knows I'm here.

Afraid to be loved too much, I tuck every
pain under the crook of my arm.

Pride has a cost and I pay the price in
loneliness.

(Don't move, hold your breath)

In the waiting room the vinyl cushion
crunches under the weight of me.

How much time do we spend trying to
overcome the history of our mothers?

How much do we unknowingly
repeat anyway?

(Thank you, you can breathe now)

TIFFANY THIELE is s a former musical theater and cruise ship performer, who spent her
younger years traveling the world. She now lives and writes in Nashville with her family and
dabbles in real estate home staging and interior design.

BODY

in the flesh / his, he left after sixty-eight years old / father of mine / is perhaps now a son a tree a bird / my brother, a body living in Seattle, used to drive my father's 2013 Sonata / a body of Hyundai / a body to a single disc CD player / a body to my dad's favorite Hindi songs / timeless old tunes / always on / always playing at very low volume / like background music / like the vibrational hum of a human being / alive like songs of a heartbeat / and just like that I am about to lose him / all over again / to take the CD out / to watch somebody come and take this car from our home / it is no match for Kelley's blue book / no match for a driver that is not my father or his son / and then my mother says do not worry, I will play the CD in my car now / as in a way to keep the beating on repeat / and I could not help but think also in a way / reincarnation

NISHI PATEL is a poet and visual artist residing in Fort Worth, Texas. Her work reflects the duality of human experiences such as grief and joy. "Body" is also found in her book, *Sometimes the Birds Come Back*. Nishi enjoys nature walks with her two daughters and husband.

I DON'T THINK OF HIM ON FATHER'S DAY

When I think of him, I think of him in vague outline,
Not the particulars, which were where things went wrong,
Just the generic, father-like things he occasionally did;
Saturday night tea in front of *The Generation Game*,
Penguin biscuits proffered from a worn plastic tub.
Going to see a man about a dog, he would say—
I allow myself these small accumulations of nothings,
Stretched thin over the place where love should be.
There are things I didn't know, until knowing them
Became the thing that defined us both.

This man who hid himself from himself,
This man whose emotional language was cars,
This man who made ball bearings, listened to Queen,
Watched *Match of the Day*, religiously,
This man who was so proud he would rather walk
Than be a passenger, this man who left marks
Upon marks upon marks, paved
With thoughts unarticulated to the last,
This man whose secrets ate him up
Until he was so full with them
He simply stopped eating and drinking,
This man for whom I had to learn
The legal definition of next of kin,
This man, who in his final days was looked after
By strangers, with a tenderness he did not afford to others.

At the funeral people I didn't know
Said things about a man I didn't know.

VICTORIA SPIRES grew her wings in the Norfolk fens, but now lives in Northampton,
a place which claims to be in the middle of England, geographically and spiritually.
Her work has been in *Flight of the Dragonfly, Comfort Zone* poetry anthology, *The Nuthatch,
Freeverse Revolution Lit*, and *The Winged Moon*.

ROOT RESORPTION

"Let's put it this way, that tooth won't be in your mouth the day you die."

The dentist confirms root resorption on my number 11, pointing to the X-ray.
He doesn't know that the tooth very well may die
with me because I've been thinking about death a
lot lately.

"The goal is to keep the tooth in your mouth as
long as we can."

The dentist lays out my options.
One being leave it be.

"Three months is a long time," I tell him with a shrug, fine with
that timeline. "No, it isn't," he responds.

The other option is a
root canal; but there
is no saving this
tooth.

"Five years is an eternity," I say in response to his
estimation. "No, it isn't," he responds.

We clearly view time differently.

Root resorption is not reversible. As is death.

I decide in that moment to let them both run their courses, naturally.
The dentist has no idea this appointment may have just saved me from myself.

ALICIA COOK is a multi-award-winning writer and mental health and addiction awareness
advocate from New Jersey. She's the poet behind the popular "poetry mixtape series," which includes
Stuff I've Been Feeling Lately, *Sorry I Haven't Texted You Back*, and *The Music Was Just Getting Good*.

A NOTE ON RUIN

Let ruin be evicted from my bones
to take shelter somewhere else.

call the ghosts out from my chest
and let them finally be at peace.

let the scorched earth of burnt bridges
grow into something other than ash.

turn my memory into something gentler
than the pressures of the past.

wash the walls of my heart
until they come up clean.

this body is no longer a memorial
for the people who chose to leave.

LAUREN LEVI is a queer poet from Birmingham, England. Her work explores the highs of love, the lows of heartbreak, and the journey to mental health recovery. Writing since her teenage years, Lauren finds poetry to be a cathartic experience to help put words to feelings which can be difficult to say out loud. This poem also appears in Levi's collection *You Bury Me*.

VETERAN

I may not have served to save my country,
but I've been served as dessert for the desire
of a soldier on leave.
Don't I deserve a Medal of Honor
for surviving, lying still while he weaponized
his own body against mine?
His bed became a battlefield, while I became
a corpse. My body froze in shell shock,
swallowing grenades and letting them detonate,
destroying my insides.
I should've known he was a mercenary,
the way he invaded me with hostility,
showing no mercy.
I was a refugee
and he was ordered
to conquer.

SARAH BLAKELY is a poet based in California whose work has appeared in several anthologies, and the 2024 issue of the *Timberline Review*. She has several collections and mainly writes about her experiences with sexual violence and healing.

I STILL HAVE ALL THE BAND-AIDS

the bloodstains start to look different as more time passes,
but they never go away.
i carry the ache as a souvenir.
i always have the map that leads back to you buried in my back pocket.
i never pull it out. i have it memorized.
i try to erase the marks you left on me,
but tattoos don't come off just because you ask them to.
your lips left behind a new permanence i had never known.
i got tired of chasing ghosts down all the wrong avenues.
i tell the wind that I don't miss you anymore.
my shadow still looks for you in October's arms.
with every year that passes, your name feels less like a freight train
and more like a postmark.
a timestamp of a memory passed.
a silhouette against an otherwise empty frame.

HALEY BUMGARDNER is a poet and avid reader living near Wilmington, NC, with her family and two dogs. Her writing carries themes of melancholy, heartbreak, and the roller coaster that is falling in love. You will often find her love-drunk, watching the sunrise on the beach.

LENT ON THE RUSCOM RIVER, 1939

They return from the obligatory mass
On a Friday They are told is "Good."
Muskrat carcasses simmer
On the wood-fired stove:

The local, plentiful water mammal They trap
Skillfully, skin diligently,
And carefully butcher
To remove the glands of musk.

This edible rodent that Their diocese
Declares They may eat
On Lenten Fridays,

That Their White, Anglo-Saxon, Protestant
Neighbours, on The Flats *du Lac Ste-Claire*,
Regard with disgust.

Shots are poured of the rye procured
By sending The One Who
Looks The Least Dark
To purchase.

Easter arrives with the festive gathering,
Le Rendez-vous, where the fiddle
And many loud, heated hands
Of Euchre are played.

The jig is danced in whirling, bright sashes.
Hats, satchels, and other items are worn,
Adorned with numerous, handsewn,
Multicoloured beads in patterns
Intricate as snowflakes.

Customs and traditions
Of The Muskrat Métis,
Dwindled down
The generations...

The very few who *are* still aware
Keep the family secret hidden
Behind wooden crosses,
Hung in every room,

While the remainder of Them,
Unknowingly,
Eat Their Identity.

ROMÉO DESMARAIS III aKa RoMeO-HoMeO ô£ tHę MâRtïÄñS >{:) (t/he/y t/he/m), an IndigiQueer/Muskrat Métis du Lac Ste-Claire spoken word performer, poet, storyteller, singer-songwriter, multimodal artist, and director of the apposite poetry performance series in London, Ontario, was showcased on The Brickyard Spoken Word YouTube Channel (2023).

SOMETIMES, I FEAR THE SANDGLASS MADE A MISTAKE

Somewhere, we're still young with
freedom for laughter and lemonade grins.
The summer air is just our home;
the sky is always close enough
to brush our toes when the swing set
creaks beneath our weight.
Would we dip into the blue,
like a gull's feet in the lake?
Is it rising or
falling when you let go?
Somewhere, we're still
young,
and we still think we see shooting
stars in the dark every time we go to
look.

Does fate gone by pile up on the shore?
Things I've lost pushed in by the tide: sand as time, time as sand, my father's
hand (in mine).

LEAH SHADLE is a poet and writer currently studying paleobiology at Bowling Green State
University. Her work is inspired by grief, hope, and a curiosity and wonder for the natural world.

PARTHENON, IF ATHENA WEREN'T THE FAVORED DAUGHTER

I have been waiting for you for what feels like my
entire life. So long that the moss has laid

claim to my feet and lichens emboss my skin in a
trail of puckered algae kissmarks. If you

were a sculptor, I am your abandoned marble, born
from between your eyes, carefully carved

into fragmentary existence then forgotten. The salt
on my cheeks dries into fissures

that crack my heart so wide not even the
winding ivy can knit my sternum back

together. I am Galatea, wondering why she was
made; Iphigenia, begging Artemis for mercy;

a girl, defined by the actions of a careless
man, indelibly rooted in time and place, waiting, waiting.

And still I wait. And forever I'll wait.

ELISE POWERS is a Seattle poet with a BA in English literature. Her work explores the human experience, spanning themes of identity, loss, and belonging. She has worked in copywriting and editing but dedicates herself to poetry. Elise enjoys sitting beachside with a book and an Americano.

BONDS

DON'T WORRY ABOUT THE BLACK TIE DRESS CODE

Don't worry about the black tie dress
code or fancy restaurant with small
portions.
I'm happy going to Burger King in our pj's at 3a.m.,
wearing paper crowns and having things our way
until the outside world rises with the day.

And when we start to feel like we're losing control,
I'll grab the car keys if you'll lock the front door,
hoping if we talk slow and eat slower
it'll keep the sun asleep a little longer.

BROOKE GOODWIN is a multi-genre writer and author of three poetry collections: *exposed, in this glass prism*, and *primality*. She is currently working on a YA action thriller novel and fantasy short story collection. Her favorite activity is buying books so her unread books don't get lonely.

IN THIS HOUSE
after Lyndsay Rush

We shake the walls with laughter. We question what we're told. We treat our colds with slippery elm and liquorice tea. We let the dandelions in the yard go to seed. We let the bees build their home. We play board games on the floor. We wear our pj's past noon. We eat breakfast for dinner. We shovel the neighbor's driveway. We pretend we're not home when the doorbell rings. We laugh when it's least appropriate, like when the world is burning and everyone disagrees. Because humour feels like a bucket of water when tossed into the fire. Because it has this beautiful way of shifting all the energy.

MICHELLE ARMITAGE is a poet living in Spruce Grove, Alberta. She finds deep purpose by sharing open and honest reflections of life in its most impactful moments. Her work explores a wide range of themes, including nostalgia, inner strength, self-reflection, resilience, and motherhood.

MELISSA ASKS ME IF I WERE AN ANIMAL
WHAT WOULD I BE

And I could say, like, a baby duck maybe.
Until I think of Laika,
the dog they sent to space
knowing she would not return.
We did not learn enough to justify the death
of the dog they say.

Or I am the shrine I keep to her
in the form of bookmarked TikToks,
you know, for when I feel like crying.
Or I am the comfortless non-love of machinery
that cradled her into molten slumber.
Maybe I am the photo of what is presumed to be
the very last Atlas lion in existence.
Or the footprints he leaves in the endless sand.

There are things that bum me out, of course,
the woman at the writing retreat
who tells a room full of strangers
that Simba was her sexual awakening,
for instance.

But more than that I am disappointed
in my ideas of what people
should keep to themselves.

I could be the drumroll of an entire colony of ants, who,
when they find themselves in line around a circular object,
form something called a

death spiral and

will march on until they drop dead, and then they march
over the tiny fallen bodies.

Not so tiny to them of course.

Perhaps I am the mirror of myself beneath my six legs,
waiting for some divine message,
for some clue to a destination I will never reach.

If I am an animal I am a waiting one.
Horizon addict I think it goes beyond the green of the grass
I will scratch at the sore spot til it bleeds, by this I mean
I will turn an almost problem into a definitely problem
so I can know what I was missing.

SOPHIE MORELLI is an Adirondacks-based poet with a bachelor's in English literature and
writing and a master's in English education from SUNY Potsdam. She was an Anne Labastille
resident and has work featured with Querencia Press. Her debut poetry collection is *Fathom*.

TULIPS V WILDFLOWERS

I feel misaligned as I walk
among the perfect rows.
The array of colors is
a baptism for my eyes,
I feel them widen.
My mom and I wonder,
do we pick them half bloomed or
closed completely?
There are fancy cameras everywhere. Capturing
perfect poses. Soon to be joined
by perfect captions.
There are people with gloves and spades, digging
the bulbs from deep in the earth.
I have no gloves or spades.
"I'm glad I wore these boots!" a woman exclaims
to her nodding friends.
I look down at my muddy sneakers.
I'm daydreaming now.
Of the time I walked through a forgotten field in
solitude, heartbroken,
with old tractor treads, gnats and mosquitos abounding.
And there they were—
the most beautiful little daisies
popping up from the ground.
There was no plan.
No pattern.
They bloomed and bloomed.
They were reckless and wild and unexpected.
They were
hope. Anchors

and compasses in a forlorn season,
a reminder that all was not lost.
"Look at that color red!" someone delights.
"It's a beautiful shade." I smile back at her.
My mom, daughter, and I have our picture taken,
collect tulips in a bucket, line up
with the crowd and wrap them
carefully.
When we get home, my Daisy arranges them
in a vase, uneven and leaning towards the sun.
I thank her.

SARA CHRISTIANSEN JEFFS is a writer, Certified Wellness Coach, and Holistic Health Practitioner. She is the founder of @dearbeautifulfriend on Instagram and the owner of Luminate Wellness Co. She hopes her writing will remind people that healing is possible, that following their heart is courageous, and that they are not alone.

IF GOD WAS TIME

the creaking clock would be a wet blanket
covering our sins
and the flowers trying so hard to bloom after winter
would be covered in blood
your hands wouldn't be lined
with every lifetime I've ever known you in
if god was time
then we would be eternal

ISABELLA LEIGH is currently studying to obtain her bachelor's in creative writing. Having
written stories as soon as she could hold a pen, she finds most inspiration in the human
relationship to nature and depth of emotion.

MY ADAM'S RIB

Generations of hatred
Gone like the wind
Love came to rescue
Two souls full of sin

Just like the church
We speak in tongues
Led by the sounds
Of our heart thumping drums

Tugging and mumbling
One caress is all it takes
I'm down on my knees
Begging for release

Oh weary soul, I have found the light
It shines and it's white, oh how bright

Thy river flowing
Thy kingdom come
This lost sheep has found its home
Forever together; never alone

WILBER A. FLORES is a writer and Coffee Master for a certain coffee company in New Jersey.
While he enjoys traveling with his wife, he also enjoys collecting vinyl records, creating mixtapes
for his family and friends, and sharing a cup or two of coffee with those close to him.

ALL MY BLUES

I press the needle to the waiting vinyl,
inviting light jazz to pour through the room

as I sway back and forth
in all my blues,

and I'm a dancer with no one to dance with,
a lover with no one to share the night with;

a performer
for an audience of none.

But it was you who told me
to save my first and last dance

and now I'm swaying alone
in this suffocating space

under the bright glow
of the dining room chandelier

because it was you
who made promises you couldn't keep—

> *but it was also you*
> *who once breathed life back into me.*

It was you who said we'd live an artist's dream:
a grand piano in the centre of our living room,

a record player in the corner wall,
and a space for your guitar.

It was you who raised hopes
only to let them fall.

It was you.
It was you.
It was you.

But it's me who's stuck with this record player
whose music floods the room,

with vinyls that collect dust
in their lonely wait for you.

It was you.
It was you.
It was you.

Oh, how I wish
it was me.

ANA DEE (Jovana Đermanović is a confessional poet from Serbia, currently based in Ontario, Canada. Her work delves into themes of love, loss, and self-exploration, capturing raw emotions with a tender voice. Her debut poetry book is *Untouched*, and her poems have been featured in various literary magazines and anthologies.

ME IN YOU

i want to crawl out of my skin when i think about all the versions of me that
exist in other people
i want to crawl into their skin and steal those versions back
to tweak them until they match the truth
my truth, at least
and then i'll silently put them back so that in case they break free
who you think i am and who i know i am could meet and recognize each other
so i could look the me in you in the eyes and just think i've found a mirror

EMILY JEAN is a singer/songwriter, photographer, and poet from Amherst, Virginia, currently
residing in Charlottesville. She began writing poetry in elementary school and continued to
develop her passion for performing and writing in college, where she studied music industry and
vocal performance with a concentration on songwriting.

SOMEONE ONCE TOLD ME

I am out with lanterns,
Looking for myself.
  - Emily Dickinson

Someone once told me not to stir up the silt that rests
at the bottom of the river.
The current hasn't flowed fast enough in years to do so.
I am here, though, with waders on,
digging blindly for myself.
Seventeen years ago, I coughed something into the water
that belonged to me, shrank in on the
hole it left below my sternum, became
flexible without it centering my bones.
Now I feel it there—a phantom.

It is a flat gray stone. It sits in the palm of my hand.
It is mine, though it gives no answers.
Only this sound, only the simple humming
of one low note.

EMILY RICHART is a writer and physical therapist living in Bend, OR. She finds awe
and connection through the conversations of life and the intricate way lives and lifetimes
communicate. A belief in the healing power of words, for both ourselves and our planet, drives her
writing and work.

THE POMEGRANATE IS A GRENADE

My mother's hands break the pomegranate open
tear two halves apart from one another
force the release of the thick red skin

In another language granada is pomegranate
the pomegranate is a grenade
the grenade breaks a mother's hands open
tears two hearts apart from one another
forces the release of thick red skin

In another language pomegranate is ruman (رمان)
Ruman is pomegranate or shell
Protective covering or explosive artillery
meticulously designed for thousands of metal shards to fly towards the target
Each fragment of the ruman has tiny seeds you don't want to miss
The fragmentation grenade is known for tearing apart limbs you will surely miss

In another language granada is pomegranate,
pomegranate is granada
In every language, we are being killed
Not the we sitting at the table here,
the we sitting under the tent, in the rain
starved from pomegranate and its sweet juice

We devour each granada, swallow the red beads of the ruman
into our stomach, pick the seeds from our teeth
and a boy in Palestine picks up
the intestines of his relative off the ground and into a plastic bag
Juice is everywhere, blood is everywhere
Hands are red and sticky, hands are red with blood

This prophetic fruit, a healing power from the gardens of paradise
became the model for gunpowder seeds and grenade shrapnel
Grenade shrapnel is also known as military confetti

I must've missed the celebration

My mom buys fifteen pomegranates awaiting my arrival,
stands at the door to greet me
A mother holds fifteen grenades awaiting her son's arrival,
the family stands at the door to greet him

he does not arrive

MAHA HASHWI is a poet and spoken word artist living in New York City. As a child of
immigrants, her work often details the experience of growing up Arab and Muslim in America.

A MOTHER / MY MOTHER

my mother / a cradle within the heart / a measure
within the noggin / weight of actions / hands of
creation / a mother, my mother / of emotions / my
mother of artistic expression / of storms that
cannot be quelled / run to the need / run to the
never / I am not, I am / a mother, my mother / apple
to the tree / falling into the shoes of / nature /
seeds from / a mother, my mother / to become of
me.

KIRA OGILVIE is a poet from the East Coast of Australia. Her first book is *Grey Linings,*
and she has had her work published in six anthologies. She lives with her husband, three young
children, and an elderly cat in her hometown.

XIPHOID, ADJ.

Our
love
hardened
over time like
the center of your
ribcage. Memories
calcified into the core
of who we were, with pain
and love all forming
the curve of the
sword. Be
careful.
Love is
sharp.

SAMUEL FAULK is a librarian/poet/writer who views words as fuel for the soul. He is the author of *The Devil's Thesaurus*. You can find "Xiphoid, adj." in its sequel, *The Angel's Addendum*. Faulk is published in several anthologies, and his local newspaper.

PRUDE SLUTS

There's nothing sexier than a legal Lolita.

Nothing more erotic than not getting arrested for dating girls who don't have anyone to compare you to.

You want an infant woman,

Woman child.

Infant woman child wife.

You want her married before she can rent a car, your blushing baby child bride.

Yeah, she *totally* came on to you.

And is there anything hotter than girls on their knees?

Looking up at you and saying "Please, Daddy, please."

"Amen." You love girls that pray.

Because you want prude sluts.

Madonna whores.

Sexy, covered, prudish whores.

Daddy's little girls.

Tell me, do you pray with them in the bedroom or fuck them in a church?

And who could resist a boss bitch?

CEOs and Stepford wives that could never bridge the wage gap.

You want housewife.

Working mom.

Doting mommy workaholic.

Oven mitts and helmets for those pesky glass ceilings.

And you know girls can have it all because you heard it on a podcast.

Non-whites need not apply.

And you're the furthest thing from shallow because there's no greater turn-on than girls who can read.

Literacy queens in negligees and knee socks.

You want smart hot.

Sexy brains.

Lusty, thinky, horny nerds.

School girls in uniforms and degrees in telling you you're brilliant. Arm candy
PhDs that like to call you senpai.

It's not racist if she's Asian, right?

Because you're an anti-racist anime fan.

Torture porn connoisseur.

You know "bitch" is a reclamation even when it's uttered by a man.

Activist for men's rights so, you call yourself an ally.

And you know your boys would never hit a girl—

No homo brotherhood.

Ugh,

You're so sexy when you're not like those other boys.

Thank God you can take a joke.

RACHEL HUH is an aspiring author who writes poetry in her free time and works as a
knowledge translation and engagement specialist at the University of Calgary by day. Public
pedagogy and social justice are the core of her professional, academic, and creative writing.

AN ODE TO SEX WORKERS

shun the guilt aside
you are breathing
you are living
no matter how many times
they try to wreck you

they call you many names
whore   kothe-wali   hooker
and you own each one of those
even when you can't own
what truly is yours

they want you
for their needs
but they don't care
about your own

you still let them in
into the most tender parts of you
let them get really close
but never enough to see inside

because that's where
your power lives
and they couldn't bear to see it

whether you chose it
or were forced into it

always
i mean always
walk with your head held high
because
you   are   beautiful
not many are
or can dare
to be
as brave
as you

TANIYA GUPTA, a poet from Punjab, India, now resides in Toronto, Canada. Her debut, *What Will People Say*, was featured in Indigo's favorite poetry list. Passionate about creating safe spaces for women to share their stories, her poems reflect on the lives that women live and the lives they don't get to live.

I REGRET NOT TELLING YOU

I was the one who cracked my heart
on the floor like an egg.
To look myself in the eye,
I changed my definition
of *villain* to your name.
I knew you were a serrated knife,
yet I licked raspberry jam
off you anyway.
I know how ridiculous it is
to blame the lion for
a human entering his den.
I knew how foolish it was
to pretend.

Half of the high
was the clichéd risk of the fall,
the other half was filling the hole
in my soul's echoing halls.
I was a foal when safety
was ripped from me.
I grew up tiptoeing around
this growing crater inside of me.
Each time I opened my mouth,
charred paths of stone led me

all
    the
        way
           down.

I'm not sure what demons of yours
mine answered, but I owe you
this dismantled illusion
of innocence.

Oh, it was me, *it—was—me*.
This is the point, you see.
I take full accountability.

And regret—nothing.

Our finest hour was when we set
each other free. Our seed burned,
but still, I grew into a tree.

AMY E. VAUGHN is a poet from New Jersey. With over fifteen years of writing experience and a
BA in English literature, her work explores womanhood, mental health, and the human experience.
She indulges in books, coffee, wandering the globe, and spending time with her cat, Baya.

NEW YEAR'S EVE

It's early in the morning
the sun hasn't reached my windows
My kids are still sleeping
and the house is quiet
I'm thankful for this stage
where they sleep later than me
I put whipped cream on my coffee
and listen to the sound of peace
Tomorrow
I am forty
Which sounds so old
although I know
in ten years I won't think so
Forty
I look at my face in the mirror
and try to tell myself
I've learned something
I try to remember
why I used to hate my nose
(That's a lie. I do remember.)
I try to pretend I'm wiser now
but I'm not sure it's true
Maybe I'm a better listener
To others, but also
to myself
When that voice in my head
sends a warning
I'm more likely to heed it
And when hateful words
fill my brain
I can hear the truth
whispering behind them
letting me know what is real
and what isn't

and I've learned
how to push the hurting
aside
So I guess that's something
I hope
in the last forty years
I've helped someone
other than myself
And I hope
I do again in the next forty

CATE MCMINN is a Minnesota-based poet. She is married with four kids, three cats, eleven dogs, and a snake. When she is not reading or writing she enjoys being part of her local community theatre, coaching high school speech, showing horses, and training sled dogs.

GOODBYE HAS A SOUND

Goodbye has a sound.
It rings like a landline in an empty
house, echoes down the hall.
Muffles our heartbeat,
the way a first snow
quiets the street.
It howls and whistles,
knocks out the power.
The sound of goodbye creates
dissonance between old and new realities,
like when our heads drop under the
water's surface and we hear everything
and nothing all at once.
Goodbye's frequency is enough to sting
the fillings we've had in our mouths since
childhood. It screeches, less like tires
turning in a parking garage and more like
incessant old radiator pipes.
It startles, like a POP
of a balloon or an
ACHOO at a funeral.
Goodbye will sing us
to sleep, then jolt us
awake, unforgivingly,
like a metal alarm clock
jumping across the nightstand.
Goodbye has a sound.

ALICIA COOK is a multi-award-winning writer and mental health and addiction awareness
advocate from New Jersey. She's the poet behind the popular "poetry mixtape series," which
includes *Stuff I've Been Feeling Lately, Sorry I Haven't Texted You Back*, and *The Music Was Just
Getting Good.*

CONTRIBUTORS

Thank you for supporting the Central Avenue Poetry Prize,
showcasing the talents of new and established poets.
Each poet featured here has earned either a cash prize or an honorarium.

Look for the third edition in spring 2026.